LET'S PLAY! LITTLE CHAMPS

FIGURE SKATING

KIM THOMPSON

NorwoodHouse Press

Cataloging-in-Publication Data

Names: Thompson, Kim, 1970-.
Title: Figure skating / Kim Thompson.
Description: Buffalo, NY : Norwood House Press, 2026. | Series: Let's play! little champs | Includes glossary and index.
Identifiers: ISBN 9781978577282 (pbk.) | ISBN 9781978577299 (library bound) | ISBN 9781978577305 (ebook)
Subjects: LCSH: Figure skating--Juvenile literature.
Classification: LCC GV850.4 T474 2026 | DDC 796.912--dc23

Published in 2026 by
Norwood House Press
2544 Clinton Street
Buffalo, NY 14224

Designer: Rhea Magaro

Photo credits: Cover, pp. 1, 14 Sergey Nivens/Shutterstock.com; p. 5 Arina P Habich/Shutterstock.com; pp. 6, 7, 12 Maria Moroz/Shutterstock.com; p. 8 PeopleImages.com - Yuri A/Shutterstock.com; p. 9 Master1305/Shutterstock.com; p. 11 FamVeld/Shutterstock.com; p. 15 GoranJakus/Dreamstime.com; p. 16 fotosparrow/Shutterstock.com; p. 17 Nigmatulina Aleksandra/Shutterstock.com; p. 18 Neyman Kseniya/Shutterstock.com; p. 19 Danmorgan12/Dreamstime.com; p. 21 LightField Studios/Shutterstock.com

Printed in the United States of America

CPSIA compliance information: Batch #CWNHP26: For further information contact Norwood House Press at 1-800-237-9932.

TABLE OF CONTENTS

What Is Figure Skating?

Figure skating is a fun activity. It is ice-skating done to music. As they glide along the ice, figure skaters do jumps, spins, and lifts.

Figure skating combines art and sport. It takes strength as well as **grace**.

Figure skating teaches balance and **coordination**. It improves a skater's **posture** and **flexibility**.

The Gear

Figure skates are the most important piece of gear. They are leather boots attached to sharp metal blades. They have extra padding around the ankle.

A toe pick is at the tip of each blade. Its sharp teeth grip the ice. This helps the skater **pivot** and jump.

At practice, figure skaters wear stretchy clothes that keep them warm. Beginners wear helmets to protect their heads during falls.

For performances, figure skaters wear beautiful costumes. They are made of stretchy fabric. They may have sparkly decorations.

At the Rink

Competitions are held at ice **rinks**. Figure skaters may perform as singles or in pairs. They skate twice: once in a short program and once in a long program.

Judges award points when skaters try difficult moves and perform them smoothly.

Skills and Jumps

Beginners learn to glide on the ice. They learn how to do a “snowplow stop” by curving their blades outward.

Figure skaters practice using the edges of their blades to move forward and back.

For edge jumps, skaters take off from one foot. An **axel** is a kind of edge jump.

A toe jump uses both feet. The toe pick on one blade helps the skater's other foot leap off the ice. A **lutz** is a kind of toe jump.

How to Be Skate-Ready

Figure skaters should eat healthy foods like fruits, vegetables, and lean meats. They should drink plenty of water. Getting enough sleep keeps them alert and ready to perform.

GLOSSARY

axel (AK-suhl): a figure skating jump with a forward takeoff, a backward landing, and one and a half turns in the air

coordination (koh-or-duh-NAY-shuhn): the ability to make different parts of your body work together smoothly

flexibility (FLEK-suh-bil-i-tee): the ability to bend easily

grace (grase): the ability to move in a smooth and beautiful way

lutz (luhts): a jump in which a figure skater takes off from the back edge of one blade using the toe pick of their free foot and makes a full turn in the air

pivot (PIV-uht): to stop in one spot and turn suddenly

posture (PAHS-chur): the way you hold your body when you stand, sit, or walk

rinks (ringks): enclosed areas with smooth surfaces that are used for skating

THINKING QUESTIONS

1. How is figure skating different from other kinds of ice-skating?
2. What is a toe pick?
3. What do figure skaters wear?
4. How do figure skaters earn points during competitions?
5. Describe one skill figure skaters learn how to do.

INDEX

ABOUT THE AUTHOR

Kim Thompson is a writer, mom, and sports fan from Columbus, Ohio. She loves to watch athletes' amazing skills on the court, field, or diamond. She believes that all kids should try out the sports that interest them and always remember to have fun!